THE WOOD ENGRAVINGS OF
RICHARD SHIRLEY SMITH

THE WOOD ENGRAVINGS OF
RICHARD SHIRLEY SMITH

SELECTED WITH AN INTRODUCTION BY
IAIN BAIN

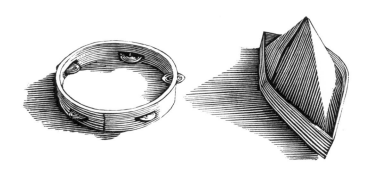

SILENT BOOKS

CAMBRIDGE

LIBELLVS ALICIAE
MATRI ARTIFICIS DONATVS,
PER QVAM OCCASIO MIRIFICA
ROMAE STVDIENDI
DATA EST

First published in Great Britain 1994
by Richard Shirley Smith
and distributed by Silent Books, Swavesey, Cambridge CB4 5RA
under their imprint

© Illustrations copyright Richard Shirley Smith 1994
© Introduction Iain Bain 1993
Richard Shirley Smith asserts all moral rights to this work

ISBN 1 85183 036 7

British Library Cataloguing-in-Publication Data
A catalogue record for this book is available from the British Library

Designed by Richard Shirley Smith
Typeset by Libanus Press, Marlborough
Printed in Great Britain by
The Alden Press Limited, Osney Mead, Oxford

Sincere thanks are extended to those who have most generously
consented to have their book plates or illustrations reproduced here

Above, Anniversary, from *A Point of Departure*, 1961, cat: 14
Opposite, Owl & Head of Pan, from *The Poems of Shelley,* 1971, cat: 179 & 183
Title page, Decoration, from *Memoirs of A London Doll,* 1967 cat: 116-131
Frontispiece, *Fatal Allegations*, acrylic on paper (detail) 1976

CONTENTS

INTRODUCTION

This selection of the wood engravings of Richard Shirley Smith represents about one third of his output over the thirty years between 1960 and 1990. It would have been possible to put together another group of equal interest from the remaining work so great is the consistency of quality, but my purpose has been to show, within the space available, a full representation of Shirley Smith's versatility and the great variety of style and subject matter which makes him so remarkable. But engraving has only been a part of his life: the fact that he is a painter of great originality, blessed with a passionate eye for detail, form, and texture, gives his engraving its strength. While so many of his contemporaries and precursors may astonish us with their virtuosity as engravers, despite his extraordinary technical skill, it is the content of his work that first catches the eye and then holds the attention in a continuous sense of discovery. At the same time responses are provoked in us which may often be more complex than were intended.

The making of the artist began when Richard Shirley Smith's family moved to Berkshire in 1939, at the beginning of the war, and he had the great good fortune to come into the circle of the composer Gerald Finzi and his wife Joy who as an artist specialised in sculpture and portrait drawing. The Finzis' championship of the arts brought many to their inspiring company: apart from the celebrated and well-known such as Ralph Vaughan Williams and Edmund Blunden,

Above, The Dark Tower & A Winter Night, from *A Point of Departure,* 1961, cat: 23 & 13
Opposite, Aspectus Mirabilis & Water into Wine, from *A Point of Departure,* cat: 25 & 24
Page 7, Classical Interior, Lady, Servants & Amorini, 1961 cat: 5
Page 6, The artist hanging the Retrospective Exhibition at the Ashmolean Museum, 1985

struggling unknowns found much support for their ambitions. It was in this milieu that Richard Shirley Smith discovered his true vocation, and as he put it himself, found he 'was able to visualise and realise images from literature'.

A chain of fortunate encounters and associations followed, all of which were of the greatest help to Shirley Smith's further development as an artist. His art master at Harrow School, Maurice Percival, who apart from becoming an important friend with a shared Catholic faith, trained him in the essential grounding of draughtsmanship and in particular in the expression of form and the handling of the fall of light on objects. Through this connection came another most fruitful friendship with the poet and painter David Jones who lived near the school and whose letters, art and writings were to become a continuing source of nourishment. Eventually it was David Jones's intervention which assisted Shirley Smith in getting a place at the Slade School of Fine Art. Here he spent four years in drawing, painting and print-making under the guidance of the painter John Aldridge, a sympathetic tutor of wide education and taste.

Soon after leaving the Slade in 1960 he married a fellow student and together, supported by their parents, they left for eighteen months' study in Italy which he had first visited when on leave from the army and had been enraptured by the splendours of Venice and the Veneto. It was here that he first took up the tools of the wood engraver: a set had been found by his wife while clearing out a drawer and she wondered if he could make use of them. Soon, without instruction, he began to master them and found much inspiration in the work of two very different engravers: the influence of the free, vigorous and painterly cutting of the Swiss artist Imre Reiner is clearly to be seen in Shirley Smith's earlier work, and Reynolds Stone's wonderfully controlled lettering continues to inspire him. The correspondence with David Jones, which began after the move to Italy, and which covered all manner of subjects, in part dealt with wood engraving after Jones had been sent some early essays in the medium – a bookplate and the group of figures in the 'Classical Interior' [p.7]: 'This cohesion business is the very devil to get . . . total unity is the *first* necessity and the *most hard*, usually, to achieve . . . I doubt whether one can just contrive a "good design" – it comes from the power of the idea incarnated in the material . . . in wood engravings in general the most satisfactory kind are those where the blacks and the whites and the greys are so "organised" or managed as to give this unity.' Nothing could have been more helpful and encouraging than to have had such letters from someone so well able to articulate the artist's struggle for truth.

The first substantial series of engravings were made for a collection of poems *A Point of Departure* by his friend Joy Finzi who had come out on a visit to Italy. Without always being directly illustrative, the seventeen blocks were cut with a wonderfully expressive freedom: the delight in the medium's possibilities is palpable, and despite an occasional want of legibility – stemming perhaps from an early uncertainty in handling tone and texture, and not helped by less than perfect printing – the mood of the poetry is most tellingly expressed. The starry chill of 'A Winter Night' seen through the window of a candle-lit room [p.8] makes a magical consonance with the verse:

> '. . .This piercing night by candlelight
> It is the cry of a child in the echoing dark
> or a sacrament with bread & wine . . .

There are many discoveries to be made in the forms and textures of the still-lifes and the distant prospects of the tiny landscapes. The book well deserves reprinting to a rather better standard.

Another product of the Roman interlude appeared in *Prospect* published in 1962 as a collection of essays, auto-biography, poetry and painting from 'the new generation'. Of the seven 'pictorial features' Shirley Smith's was that of a lone wood-engraver amongst six photographers: his record of the ancient Rome he had studied with such passion at the British School has so much better stood the test of time. The texts he wrote to accompany his work perfectly reflect his pre-occupations, as for example his piece on the 'Ruined Church' [p.23]: [The Cosmati's] sense of geometric patterns set off against, perhaps, intricate edgings of gilded tessere and their use of green- or purple-flecked stone with different neutral tones is one of the greatest joys of Rome....The sun on the rough, off-white tufa slabs and brickwork of the Roman ruins makes an unforgettable harmony with blue sky, bay and laurel'.

Two other engravings of this earlier period, shown on p.26, 'Madonna and

Child' and 'An Angel visits Anna and Joachim', continue to display a vigorous spontaneity and an obvious delight in the medium's possibilities. It is particularly interesting to see how, as his work progresses, Shirley Smith begins to establish his own distinctive vocabulary for interpreting the exquisitely finished gouache drawings in whites and greys which it has always been his custom to prepare on the woodblock surface. But never does he arrive at purely mechanical and repetitive conventions so evident in the work of the nineteenth-century trade engravers.

Above, *Temple of Antoninus & Faustina*, Roman Forum, 1961, cat: 8
Below, In Passing, from *A Point of Departure*, 1967 cat: 21

Opposite, Dedication, from *A Point of Departure*, 1961, cat: 11
Whither, from *A Point of Departure*, cat: 17

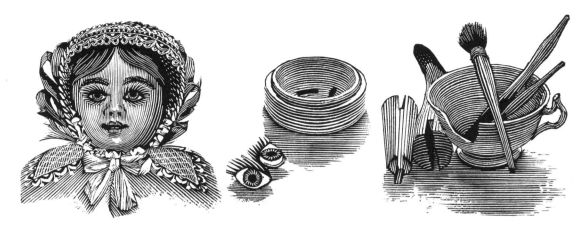

Chapter headings, for *Memoirs of a London Doll*, Andre Deutsch 1967, cat: 116-131

Chapter headings for *The Gourmet's Garden*, Faber & Faber, 1964, cat: 44-53

Three of twelve heads for *Lord Chesterfield's Letters*, Folio Society, 1973, cat: 217-228

During the six years it took to find a publisher for *A Point of Departure*, a visit to Anthony Gross, Shirley Smith's teacher of etching at the Slade, led to introductions into the publishing trade, and a number of commissions for book illustration came to him from Faber & Faber, Oxford University Press, Wine and Food Magazine and Burns & Oates. Those for Faber, chapter heads in *The Darkening Green*, are shown on p.28 and the sleeping cat, the wild rose, the harvest mouse, butterflies and beehives display particularly well his gift for the decorative reflection of the mood of a text. As it was never possible to find enough of this kind of work, a living had to be earned by part-time lecturing while at Highgate, followed by four years of teaching at Marlborough College Art Departmnent. Here he worked with Mark Wickham, a former contemporary at the Slade and gained broadening experience from additional activity such as theatre design and construction, and photography.

The publishing of the Finzi poems in 1967 was eventually undertaken by Raymond Lister's Golden Head Press in Cambridge – an introduction made by Laurence Whistler the glass engraver, whose brother Rex's work has so much inspired Shirley Smith. Of an earlier generation, and tragically killed towards the end of the second World War, Rex Whistler likewise trained at the Slade, went to the British School in Rome, was enchanted by the Baroque, worked on bookplates, book illustration and the painting of murals. This once prompted Shirley Smith to observe that Whistler seemed to have achieved everything in a short life that he himself had struggled for a lifetime to emulate. But it cannot be said that the younger man's work is in any way imitative: he has too much originality of invention, and there is rather more of a subversive and surrealistic edge to his work – particularly in his paintings, many of which reflect his delight in the cheerful anarchy of the *Commedia dell'Arte*. Something of this can be seen in a detail of *Fatal Allegations* reproduced here as a frontispiece, in the 'Two Fantastics' [p.20] and in the four engravings for the Oxford University Press's 'Cupid's Progress' commissioned for the quarterly *Periodical* in 1970 [pp. 38 and 39]. In the latter a sense of mystery and ambiguity is pervasive: will the maturing cupid be shorn of his other wing, and will his soul, sleeping under the shroud, wake to animate the contemplative gaze of the man and girl?

The decorative headpieces engraved for three books published between 1964 and 1973 – *Memoirs of a London Doll*, *The Gourmet's Garden*, and *Chesterfield's Letters* – some of which are displayed together for comparison [opposite], provide us with a fine example of Shirley Smith's capacity to adapt his manner to subject matter: bold and vigorous linear simplicity for the doll's memoirs, rich and strongly lit forms for the gourmet's fruits, and a great variety of far from conventional short-stroked impressionistic cutting to convey a slightly sinister sensuality in the eighteenth-century portraits.

Raymond Lister's publishing of *A Point of Departure* brought Shirley Smith's work to the attention of the distinguished typographer John Dreyfus who was at that time designing a series of handsome editions of British poets for the Limited Editions Club of New York, and from him came the commission to engrave

Above, Keats's Deathmask with Flowers in Rome, from *The Poems of Shelley,* cat: 167
Above right, Three engravings from Peter Bell the Third, from *The Poems of Shelley,* 1971
   cat: 202 '. . . bowled to Hell in the Devil's Chase'
   cat: 204 '. . . did perk and peer till he saw Peter dead or napping . . .'
   cat: 206 '. . . with loose fat smile the willing wretch sat winking there'

Opposite, Horsenden Manor, 1976, cat: 237a

illustrations for Stephen Spender's edition of Shelley's poems, eventually published in 1971. The number of blocks required provided a real opportunity to do
the text justice and the book that resulted is quite the most successful of Shirley
Smith's collaborations as an illustrator. The marriage of subject and image, the
harmony of wood-engraving and typography in a most handsome tall format,
perfectly demonstrate the advantages of working in sympathy with subject matter and designer, with unrestrained freedom to seek inspiration in the text. The
work came at an unhappy time, yet the break-up of his marriage and an emo-
tionally disturbed life may have enhanced the artist's response to Shelley's
verse. As he said to John Dreyfus, he allowed the poems 'to make pictures in my

mind' and then engraved them 'in such a style that Shelley himself would find no difficulty in looking at them'. Later Dreyfus remarked 'I marvel afresh at the ability with which he was able to render intricate details of architecture, landscape, seascape, flora, fauna, and the human face – all with equal mastery, and with an astonishing control of perspective, and the lighting of different planes'.

Only twenty of the forty-six engravings can be shown here and on pages 30-37, yet in them we see most clearly how much had been absorbed in the travels to Rome, to Padua and to Venice. Sometimes there is rather less chiaroscuro than in the earlier work and more consciousness of surface texture and the fall of light on warm stone, of time passing and of time stood still. In writing of his work on a series of film strips he prepared on the villas of the Veneto, Shirley Smith speaks of these influences and of his fascination with the magnificent buildings, sculptures and frescos of Palladio, Vittoria, Veronese and the Tiepolos 'in every stage of romantic decay revealed by Italian sun and projected shadows . . . ballrooms had become barns and rustic rakes leaned on the busts of the Caesars . . .'. It is not easy to pick out engravings from the *Shelley* for particular attention, and more than most they need to be seen in context to be fully appreciated, but certainly their sheer variety should be remarked upon – from the dreamlike death-mask of Keats [opposite] and the small racing coach and grotesques to the exquisite portraits of young women, [pp.33 & 34], the emblematic garland [p.36] and the moonlit Endymion [p.37]

During the 1970s several particularly fine house portraits were engraved for use on writing paper, and although they could not possibly have engaged him to the same degree as the *Shelley*, Shirley Smith's powerful sense of design, control of perspective and feeling for landscape context never deserts him. One of these can be seen here and two are shown on p.42.

Bookplate for A.K. Petford, 1979, cat: 244
Bookplate for Auberon Waugh, 1978, cat: 242

In the decade that followed, time much taken up with painting and mural work, he was nevertheless able to produce a noble group of bookplates, the most arresting of which was engraved very appropriately for a leading scholar of the subject, Brian North Lee [p.43]. So often bookplates attempt to include far too many of the owners' diverse interests, but here the simple but powerful theme of antiquity in crumbling decay, overgrown by ever vigorous nature, has been handled with great mastery. The selection of fourteen shown [pp.43-9] again display Shirley Smith's extraordinary versatility, from the splendidly decorative cartouche for Adrian Sassoon to the elegant heraldic devices for the Listers and for John Bullitt's Oak Hill, all enhanced by the most accomplished letter cutting. Benoît Junod's cats add a delightful liveliness to the elegant coat of arms sculpted on the stone pedestal, and the Ely's Siamese cat sitting by an elaborate Chilean wooden stirrup has a wonderful sense of exotic mystery. In the commissioning of my own larger plate, it was particularly interesting to observe Shirley Smith's response to my request for a distant seascape in which my grandfather's ship sailed: in the need to find something on which his skills and imagination could feed, his own searches produced a reference to the extraordinary rock formations on the Black Isle near the ship's home port of Cromarty, while the introduction of the distant castle of Eilean Donan, actually on the western

[16]

coast of Scotland, fortuitously made a link with my grandmother's native heath. The plate for Auberon Waugh shown [opposite] contains skilfully reticent references to the titles of two of his books *The Foxglove Saga* and *Consider the Lilies*, and Amanda K.Petford's emblematic plate is brilliantly designed with ribbons and leafage uniting four very different objects in great harmony. An alternative painted block prepared for Mrs Keswick's plate is shown below beside a print from the one finally engraved. This is interesting on two counts: we can compare the exquisite finish of the drawing on the wood with the tool marks used to interpret tonality and texture, and we can also see that every element in the design has been slightly shifted to improve the composition.

1985 was a significant year for Shirley Smith's reputation as an engraver. Almost all his engravings were shown together in the separate Eidon Gallery during his retrospective at the Ashmolean Museum, and copies of all of them were bought for the permanent collection. The Cuckoo Hill Press's *Selected*

Bookplate for Mrs H. Keswick, 1988, cat: 284
Monochrome preparatory study for the above

[1 7]

Above, Arms of Pope Leo X, from *Messer Pietro Mio*, 1985, cat: 276

Below, Lucrezia mourns Pope Alexander VI, from *Messer Pietro Mio*, cat: 280

A.   The design is proposed on the block in thin gouache and pencil, and the tools cut through into the wood in as slow, detailed and varied a manner as can be devised

B.   All white is cut away, black left standing and greys interpreted in various textures. The paint is wiped away with a damp cloth, and when dry, the block is rolled with stiff black ink. This is an exciting moment and the printing ink shows up well against the pale wood.

C.   Washing ink off with white spirit is delayed as long as possible, as from then on, the powder has to be applied and removed in order to see the cutting, as here for finishing touches.

Above, Two Fantastics, 1984, cat: 283
Opposite, Small Bookplate, for Iain Bain, 1983, cat: 253

Engravings had just come out, and in Lawrence Whistler's introduction, his observation that the artist's way ahead lay in 'the fantastic and the poetical', was echoed by Sir Roy Strong in his *Financial Times* article reviewing the Retrospective. In the same year Michael Mitchell published at his Libanus Press a most beautifully produced letterpress printing of a translation of the sixteenth-century letters of Lucrezia Borgia and Pietro Bembo, *Messer Pietro Mio,*with wood engravings by Shirley Smith. Without having quite the harmony of engraving and text which runs so successfully through the *Shelley*, there are nevertheless many extremely handsome spreads. There are emblematic, decorative and interpretive engravings of the finest. The sorrow of Lucrezia, weeping beside her father's elaborate tomb [p.19] is most tenderly expressed in every line of her body; in contrast the table laden with symbols of death and discarded helmets, masks and mitres, has about it an eerie stillness, interrupted only by the running of the sand in the hour-glass [p.50]. All the work for the book has been engraved in a controlled and highly finished manner which demands the utmost of a print-er's skill. Too loose an ink would fill the stippled grounds to be seen, for instance, in the heraldic device above on page 51. To maintain the correct tonal relation-ships, elaborate overlays of tissue have to be prepared to bring increased pres-sure to bear on the darker tones, and all this has to be done with the utmost precision on the tympan or platen that carries the paper to the inked printing surface. The progress of the engraving of one of these blocks has been recorded on page 18 – a progress in which Shirley Smith once described himself as 'crawling like an ant' over the block's surface.

Though not strictly within the definition of wood engraving, I have included in the selection, examples from two privately printed books: *The Prince and the Puppeteer* [front endpaper] and *Hero and Leander.* [pp.64-65 and back end-paper] These splendidly vigorous linocuts with their freedom and sense of design on the page, show how well Shirley Smith accommodates himself to the larger scale and how well the fantastic and the sensual work on his imagination.

Now that other interests prevail, particularly in painting, Shirley Smith's wood engraving has come to a stop, if not permanently, then for the forseeable future. The work is demanding technically, and though an image can appear large on the block when working close up, the strain on hand and eye is considerable. Nevertheless a number of commissions for letterheads, bookplates and the dec-oration of books have continued to appear: drawing with the pen on a larger scale for subsequent reduction has been the means of producing them. On p.57 a group can be seen where the dotted manner, although without the sharp precision of the engraved work, has a special quality of its own.

The linocuts and drawings have been grouped together in a separate section, together with various designs shown in the typographic context for which they were made. I hope that the discerning will be encouraged by the latter examples to seek out the original books. Some signed proofs are still available from the artist himself and no serious admirers of the art of wood engraving should deny themselves the opportunity to acquire original prints from one of its most remarkable practitioners.

THE WOOD ENGRAVINGS

Preparatory painting for a bookplate, see page 43

Sta Maria del Popolo and The Cosmati in Rome, 1961 from *Prospect*, cat: 31 and 32

The Piercéd Side, cat: 18 and In That Place, cat: 16
from *A Point of Departure*, 1961

Meet and Part, cat: 19 and The Traveller, cat: 12
from *A Point of Departure*, 1961

[25]

Madonna and Child with Cockatoo, 1963 cat: 38
An Angel visits Anna and Joachim, 1961, cat: 6

[26]

Kitchen Table for *Wine & Food*, 1964 cat: 75
Portrait of Teilhard de Chardin for Burns & Oates, 1965, cat: 81

[27]

3

4

5

6

7

The Artist's Cats, 1981, cat: 252
Portrait of Pépé, 1980, cat: 245

Opposite, 5 Chapter headings for *The Darkening Green*
Faber & Faber, 1964, cat: 58 to 67

From *The Poems of Shelley* The Limited Editions Club of New York, 1971
Above, The Pyramid of Cestus near the Protestant Cemetery, Rome, cat: 173
Shelley at the Baths of Caracalla, Rome, cat: 165

Opposite, Monuments in the Desert (Part I, The Confessional Poet) cat: 172
Ariel, Shelley's drifting boat, cat: 166

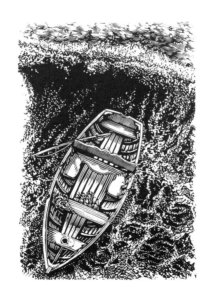

From, *The Poems of Shelley*, 1971

Opposite, Flowery Wreath (Elegy on the Death of Adonis) cat: 180
Moths and Moon (Part II Love) cat: 192

Above, Draped pensive woman (Part VII Mutability) cat: 189
Girl offering chalice (The Triumph of Life) cat: 199

From, *The Poems of Shelley,* 1971

With a Guitar, to Jane (Part V The Invitation) cat: 169
Portrait of Jane Williams (The Pine Forest of the Cascine) cat: 168

From, *The Poems of Shelley*, (both from Julian & Maddalo)
Dark tower in water against sunset, cat: 190
Reclining Girl's head with flowers, cat: 198

From, *The Poems of Shelley,* 1971

Aphrodite in a Greek Temple, (Part VIII Translations) cat: 191
Wreathed urn, cone spear and curtain, (Adonais) cat: 182

From, *The Poems of Shelley*, 1971
Ozymandias, (Part IV Politics) cat: 187
Endymion in moonlight, (Epipsychidion) cat: 196

CUPID'S PROGRESS or The Four Seasons
1970, cat: 161 to 164

Four pearwood cover designs for the Oxford University
Press quarterly *The Periodical*

Two Engravings for The Gruffyground Press in 1977
Six Hampshire Epitaphs cat: 240 and *The Closed Door* cat: 239

Opposite, Two Engravings for *Vines*, Rocket Press in 1984
Thais, cat: 257 and Girl's head cat: 258

Above, Combe Florey House for Auberon Waugh, 1977, cat: 229
Greens Old Farm for Martin Trowell, 1976, cat: 237 B

Opposite, Bookplate for Brian North Lee, 1984, cat: 259
Bookplate for John Retallack, 1974, cat: 232

BRIAN
NORTH LEE
F·S·A

Bookplate for Lord Rothschild, 1975, cat: 215
Bookplate for Anne Stevens, 1985, cat: 255

Opposite, Bookplate for Iain Bain, 1980, cat: 247
Bookplate for Benoît Junod, 1975, cat: 256

ADRIAN SASSOON

Bookplate for Adrian Sassoon, 1980, cat: 248
Bookplate for Mr & Mrs Robert Ely, 1980, cat: 249

Bookplate for John Loch, 1983, cat: 254
Bookplate for P & D Colnaghi, 1980, cat: 246

Bookplate for Raymond & Pamela Lister, 1984, cat: 262
Bookplate for Oswald Cheung, 1984, cat: 261

OAK HILL

Bookplate for John C. Bullitt, 1984, cat: 260
Bookplate for David Profumo, 1984, cat: 263

PREFACE

From *Messer Pietro Mio*, Libanus Press, 1985
Preface, cat: 277 and Triumph of Death, cat: 279

From *Messer Pietro Mio*, Libanus Press, 1985
Bembo Funerary Arms, cat: 272 and Este Tomb, cat: 278

From *Messer Pietro Mio,* 1985, Putti playing with Helmet and Thunderbolt, cat: 270
Pietro Bembo, cat: 274 and Lucrezia Borgia, cat: 273

Five decorations for *Messer Pietro Mio*, 1985
Cornucopias, cat: 268, Flower decoration, cat: 265, Heart pendant, cat: 281
Scallop, cat: 282 and Altar (Est animum), cat: 267

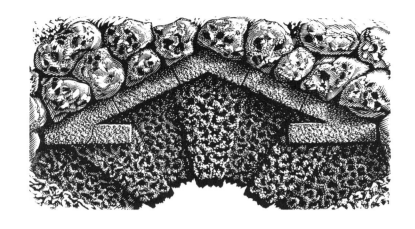

Chapter headings for Julian Berry, St Barnabas Press
Stourhead, Fonthill Splendens & Painshill 1989, cat: 286, 287 and 285

LINE DRAWINGS
LINO CUTS & ILLUSTRATIONS
WITH TYPE

Mr and Mrs Lionel Conway
request the pleasure of your company at

THE DORIC VILLA
19 York Terrace East
Regent's Park London NW1

on Thursday 7th December

The mural decoration & preparatory studies
by Richard Shirley Smith may be seen

Drinks   7 pm to 9 pm   R S V P

Decorated rule for Folio Society Prospectus, 1965, cat: 80
The original layout for Doric detail, 1978, cat: 243 B

TWO EXHIBITIONS
1st to 27th November, 1976
AT THE UNIVERSITY OF DURHAM

Richard Shirley Smith

Collingwood College
SOUTH ROAD DURHAM

PAINTINGS, COLLAGES & ENGRAVINGS
open daily from 9 a.m. to 10p.m.

YOU ARE INVITED TO THE PRIVATE VIEW ON
SUNDAY 31ST OCT. BETWEEN 8 P.M. & 10.30 P.M.

University Library
PALACE GREEN DURHAM

*ILLUSTRATED BOOKS, PROOFS
& BLOCKS*
open weekdays from 9 a.m. onwards

All sales inquiries to David Burnett
33 Hastings Ave. Tel. Durham 3039 (Office 61262)

The Artist will show slides and talk
about his work to the
Durham Fine Arts Society
Monday 29th November at 8.30p.m.

ELVET RIVERSIDE NEW ELVET DURHAM
The Public are welcome

SIR GEORGE TAYLOR
EX LIBRIS
AD
STANLEY SMITH
HORTICULTURAL TRUST

Humphrey Stone is the typographer for the
Sir George Taylor bookplate cat: 233 and the
Durham University card cat: 238

Libanus Press logo, 1975, cat: 235

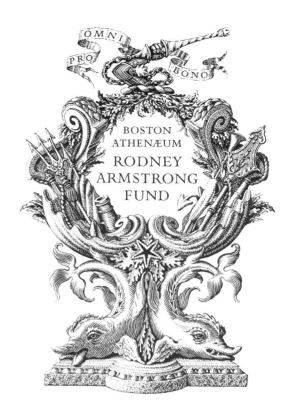

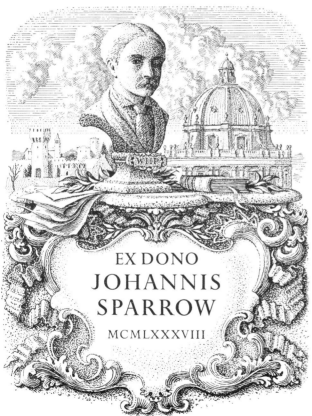

Bookplate for Benoît Junod, 1993
Bookplate for Brasenose College, Oxford, 1989

Bookplate for Rodney Armstrong Fund, 1992
Bookplate for Charles C. Dickinson III, 1993

Now is come a darker day,
And thou soon must be his prey,
If the power that raised thee here
Hallow so thy watery bier.
A less drear ruin then than now,

With thy conquest-branded brow
Stooping to the slave of slaves
From thy throne, among the waves
Wilt thou be, when the sea-mew
Flies, as once before it flew,
O'er thine isles depopulate,
And all is in its ancient state,

THE POEMS OF
PERCY BYSSHE SHELLEY

Selected, edited, and introduced by
STEPHEN SPENDER

Illustrated with wood engravings by
RICHARD SHIRLEY SMITH

Printed for the members of
THE LIMITED EDITIONS CLUB
at the University Printing House
Cambridge: 1971

John Heath-Stubbs

BUZZ BUZZ *Ten Insect Poems*

with a wood engraving by
Richard Shirley Smith

THE GRUFFYGROUND PRESS · SIDCOT
MCMLXXXI

These two Title Pages were designed by Michael Mitchell
The previous pages 58 and 59 were designed by John Dreyfus

Messer Pietro Mio

The letters between
LUCREZIA BORGIA
& PIETRO BEMBO

1503 to 1519

Translation & Preface
HUGH SHANKLAND

Wood engravings
RICHARD SHIRLEY SMITH

Libanus Press

1985

SIR ROGER IN CHURCH

⟶ ❧◯❧ ⟵

'Αθανάτους μὲν πρῶτα θεούς, νόμῳ ὡς διάκειται, τίμα.*
PYTHAGORUS

I am always very well pleased with a Country *Sunday*; and think, if keeping holy the Seventh Day were only a human Institution, it would be the best Method that could have been thought of for the polishing and civilizing of Mankind. It is certain the Country-People would soon degenerate into a kind of Savages and Barbarians, were there not such frequent Returns of a stated Time, in which the whole Village meet together with their best Faces, and in their cleanliest Habits, to converse with one another upon indifferent Subjects, hear their Duties explained to them, and join together in Adoration of the supreme Being. *Sunday* clears away the Rust of the whole Week, not only as it refreshes in their Minds the Notions of Religion, but as it puts both the Sexes upon appearing in their most agreeable Forms, and exerting all such Qualities as are apt to give them a Figure in the Eye of the Village. A Country-Fellow distinguishes himself as much in the *Church-yard*, as a Citizen does upon the *Change*, the whole Parish-Politicks being generally discuss'd in that Place either after Sermon or before the Bell rings.

My Friend Sir ROGER being a good Churchman, has beautified the Inside of his Church with several Texts of his own chusing: He has likewise given a handsome Pulpit-Cloth, and railed in the Communion-Table at his own Expence. He has often told me that at his coming to his Estate he found his Parishioners very irregular; and that in order to

* First honour the immortal gods as the law decrees.

Wood-engraved vignette and decorated rule
from *Sir Roger de Coverly*, The Folio Society, 1967 cat: 85 to 115

SOLILOQUY OF THE SPANISH CLOISTER

Gr-r-r – there go, my heart's abhorrence!
    Water your damned flowerpots, do!
If hate killed men, Brother Lawrence,
    God's blood, would not mine kill you!
What? your myrtle-bush wants trimming?
    Oh, that rose has prior claims –
Needs its leaden vase filled brimming?
    Hell dry you up with its flames!

At the meal we sit together:
    *Salve tibi!** I must hear
Wise talk of the kind of weather,
    Sort of season, time of year:
Not a plenteous cork-crop: scarcely
    Dare we hope oak-galls, I doubt:
What's the Latin name for 'parsley'?
    What's the Greek name for Swine's Snout?*

8

Cartouche reduced from a line drawing
from *Browning's Dramatic Monologues*, The Folio Society, 1991

HERO AND
LEANDER

Engravings on lino from *Hero & Leander* (actual size), 1969, cat: 143-160

All the engravings illustrated in this book have a number from the catalogue below in the captions. Height before width in cm. Boxwood engravings unless otherwise stated. The numbers which refer to engravings in published books (e.g. A Point of Departure (11-27) follow the page order of each book. Separate titles and enumeration (e.g. The Poems of P.B. Shelley 165-210) are given to those engravings of which there were limited editions.

1 Inscription TU ES PETRUS 15.75 x 11.75 1960

2 Inscription QUOMODO CANTABIMUS 7.75 x 15.5 1960

3 Design from Roman sarcophagus 9.5 x 11.5 1961

4 Three dancing nymphs 11 x 8.5 1961

5 Classical interior, lady, servants, & amorini 12.5 x 9 1961

6 Anna and Joachim 7.75 x 10 1961

7 Bookplate for Juliet Shirley Smith 6.5 x 5.5 1961

8 Temple of Antoninus and Faustina 7.75 x 10.75 1961

9 Bookplate for Michael Q. Smith 5 x 8.5 1961

10 Vines 6.5 x 7.5 1961
Cover design for *When April Came* by M. Burtch, Novello

11-27 17 engravings for *A Point of Departure* by J. Finzi, Golden Head Press, engraved 1961, published 1967

28-32 5 engravings for *Prospect*, edited by Roger Bannister, Hutchison, 1962

33 Bookplate for Timothy Harman 4 x 7 1962

34 Bookplate for Tim Bottaci 4.5 x 5 1962

35 PAX seal for Valentine Ackland 2 x 1.75 1962

36 Madonna and Child with candle and wreath 7.5 x 7.25 1962

37 Madonna and Child 7 x 4.25 1963

38 Madonna and Child with Cockatoo 9.5 x 8 1963

39 St Teresa of Avila 6 x 5 1963
Enlarged for cover for The Great Teresa by Elizabeth. Hamilton, Burns and Oates (Universe Books edition)

40 Shipwreck 10.75 x 8.5 1963
Enlarged to 22.5 x 16.5 for dustjacket of *Pandora's Last Voyage* by G. Rawson, Longmans, 1963

41 Ivory crozier 10 x 9 1963. Limited edition of 100
Dustjacket design for *The English Church 1000-1066* by F. Barlow, Longmans, 1963

42 St Cuthbert's Cross 3.75 x 3.75 1963

43 St Francis 10.75 x 7.5 1963. Limited edition of 100
Dustjacket design for *The Writings of St Francis of Assisi*, Burns and Oates, 1963

44-53 10 engraved decorations for *The Gourmet's Garden* by D. Bartrum, Faber & Faber, 1964
Merivale Edition of 500 in 1986

54-57 4 engraved decorations for *To any Christian* by a Benedictine of Stanbrook, Burns and Oates, 1964

58-67 10 engravings for *The Darkening Green* by E. Clarke, Faber & Faber, 1964. Limited edition of 100

68 Dustjacket design 12 x 8.5 1964
For *Helmet and Wasps* by M. Mott, Andre Deutsch, 1964

69 Bookplate for C.D. Gomperts 6.75 x 5 1964

70 Dustjacket design 7 x 12 1964
For *The Trial of Thomas More* by E.E. Reynolds, Burns and Oates, 1964

71 Bookplate for Leonard Clark 4.5 x 3.5 1964

72 Portrait of R. Vaughan Williams 4.5 x 3 1964
For Composers' Guild of Great Britian

73 Crab apples and jug 4.75 x 7 1964
Limited edition, circa 1965

74 Apples and pear 4 x 3 1964
Used as decoration of *Sapient Pig* menu 1984

75 Kitchen table 7 x 12.5 1964 Pearwood
Illustration for article by Douglas Bartrum in *Wine and Food Magazine*, 1964. Limited edition of 30, 1979

76 Christmas card (table top) 15.75 x 10.5 1964 Pearwood

77 Daphne 11 x 15.5 1965 Pearwood
Dustjacket design for *Metamorphoses* by Ursula Vaughan Williams, Duckworth, 1965

78 Cover design 14.5 x 12 1965
For *False Colours* by G. Heyer, Longmans, 1965

79-80 2 engravings for a prospectus, The Folio Society, 1965. Headpiece 5.75 x 9.5 and Decorated rule 1.5 x 9.75

81 Portrait of Teilhard de Chardin 9 x 12.75 Pearwood
Dust jacket design for *The Faith of Teilhard de Chardin* by H. de Lubac, Burns and Oates, 1965

82 Portrait of Erasmus 7 x 8 1965
Dustjacket design for *Thomas More and Erasmus* by E.E. Reynolds, Burns and Oates, 1965 (paste up)
Portrait of Erasmus. Limited edition of 30

83 Christmas card (with scales) 17 x 11 1965 Pearwood

84 Portrait of Margaret Clitherow 12.5 x 11.5 1965 Pearwood
Dustjacket design and frontispiece for *Margaret Clitherow* by M. Claridge, Burns and Oates, 1965

85-115 31 engravings for *Sir Roger de Coverly* by Addison and Steele, Folio Society, 1967

116-131   16 engravings on pearwood for *Memoirs of a London Doll* by R.H. Horne, Andre Deutsch, 1967

132   The Old Rectory, Chilton Foliat, for Auberon Waugh   6.25 x 10.5   1967

133   Engraving for *Garland, an anthology*, Golden Head Press, 1968

134   Upper Upham, for John Anstey   6.5 x 9.5   1968   Limited edition of 60, 1980

135   Venetian Cartouche   37 x 25.5   1968.   Engraved on Lino (unpublished)

136   Rhinoceros in Venice   37 x 25.5   1968. Engraved on Lino (unpublished)

137-142   6 engravings on lino for *The Prince and the Puppeteer* by J.C. Bretherton, Compton Press, 1969

143-160   18 engravings on lino for *Hero and Leander* by D. Burnett, engraved 1969, published privately in an edition of 200, 1975

161-164   Cupid's Progress, 4 engravings, each   9.5 x 12   1970   Pearwood
Cover designs for The Periodical, Oxford University Press, 1970, Spring, Summer, Autumn and Winter issues
Limited edition of 30 of each engraving

46 engravings for *The Poems of P. B. Shelley*, selected by Stephen Spender, Limited Editions Club of New York, 1971
Limited editions of 25 of the following engravings:

165   Shelley at Baths of Caracalla   pIX   7.25 x 10

166   Shelley's boat   p63   7 x 3.25

167   Keats's deathmask with flowers in Rome   p109   9 x 7

168   Portrait of Jane Williams   p267   4 x 5.5

169   Jane with guitar in pinewood   p257   9 x 6

170   Santa Maria della Salute, Venice   p132   11.5 x 5.5

171   Mont Blanc with broken pine trees   p121   5.75 x 7.75

172   Monuments in desert   p1   7.5 x 6.25

173   Pyramid near Protestant Cemetery, Rome   p192   4 x 9

174   Butterflies on flower   p73   7.5 x 6

175   Grasshopper   p77   3.5 x 5

176   Matted tree root   p159   2.5 x 7.5

177   Spider   p6   2.5 x 3

178   Toad   p150   3.5 x 2.75

179   Owl   p149   3 x 3.5

180   Flowery wreath   p308   6 x 9

181   Flowers and skull in basket   Title page   4.5 x 6

182   Wreathed urn, cone spear & curtain   p180 5.5 x 7.75

183   Head of Pan   p141   5 x 4

184   Vignette   p15   2.5 x 4.5

185   William Shelley as a small boy with toy   p59   5.5 x 5

186   Contessina Emilia Viviani   p82   5 x 3.25

187   Two vast and trunkless legs of stone   p195   9 x 6.5

188   Crown & mitre with fluttering monsters   p273   9 x 6.5

189   Draped pensive woman in Roman ruins   p295   9 x 5.75

190   Dark tower in water against sunset   p20   9 x 6.5

191   Aphrodite in Greek temple   p304   9 x 6

192   Moths and moon   p79   9 x 6

193   Volcano and islanded lake   p54   6.75 x 8.25

194   Veiled maid in jungle   p42   5.5 x 7.75

195   Moon behind cloud   p115   6 x 4.75

196   Endymion in moonlight   p91   5.75 x 7.5

197   Anarchy – skeleton rider   p241   7.75 x 5.5

198   Reclining girl's head with flowers   p33   4.5 x 6.25

199   Girl offering chalice   p288   3 x 7.5

200   Dead girl in the rain   p299   3.5 x 5.5

201   Lattice window open in moonlight   p220   3.25 x 5

202   The Devil's chase   p208   3.25 x 5

203   Death of Liberty   p227   3.25 x 5

204   Devil at death bed   p205   3.25 x 5

205   Yawning head   p230   3.25 x 5

206   Smiling face   p213   3.25 x 5

No limited edition of the following:

207   The parson from the casement leapt   p201   3.25 x 5

208   The king would dress an ape up in his crown   p173   2.5 x 7.75

209   Girl's head   p104   3.25 x 4.75

210   Woman and hackney cab   p13   4.25 x 6.5

211-214   4 engravings on lino as menu headings for the Hyde Park Hotel   c: 7 x 23   1972

215   Bookplate for Lord Rothschild   6.5 x 8   1973

216   Doves at Ham for Lord Rothschild   First state 5 x 9.75   1973

217-228   12 portrait engravings for *Letters to his son* by the Earl of Chesterfield, Folio society,   1973 Pearwood
Limited editions of 60 of 2 men   p19   5.75 x 9.5
                                                    2 women   p79 5.5 x 9.75

229   Combe Florey House for Auberon Waugh   6.25 x 10.25   1973

230   Cove House for Giles FitzHerbert   5.25 x 7.5   1973

231   Bookplate for James Ley Wilson   8 x 6   1974   Limited edition of 60

232   Bookplate for John Retallack   4.25 x 9.5   1974   Limited edition of 80

233   Bookplate for Sir George Taylor   9.5 x 7   1974   Limited edition of 60

234   Christmas card   17.5 x 13.5   1974   Lino

235   Cone and ribbons logo for the Libanus Press   2.5 x 2.5   1975

236   Bookplate for Michael Mitchell   10.5 x 8.75   1975   Limited edition of 35. Second edition of 100 (Roman numerals)

237a Horsenden Manor for Mrs J. Gourlay   6 x 10   1976
Limited edition of 60

237b Greens Old Farm for Martin Trowell 1976   6.5 x 9
Limited edition of 27

238 Nymph and Pulcinella   5 x 7.5   1976
For Durham exhibition card. Limited edition of 50

239 Frontispiece   9 x 6.5   1977
For *The Closed Door* by James Reeves, Gruffyground Press, 1977. Limited edition of 60. Second edition of 100 (Roman numerals)

240 Churchyard   4 x 7.5   1977
For *Six Hampshire Epitaphs*, Gruffyground Press, 1977. Limited edition of 50. Second edition of 50 (Roman numerals)

241 Bookplate for Michael Riviere   6.5 x 8.25   1978
Pearwood. Limited edition of 60

242 Bookplate for Auberon Waugh   9.5 x 7.25   1978
Limited edition of 100

243a Bookplate for Mr and Mrs R. Walker   10.25 x 7   1978

243b Doric detail for invitation card   8.25 x 4.25   1978
Limited edition of 60

244 Bookplate for A.K. Petford   7.25 x 5.5   1979
Limited edition of 100

245 Portrait of Pépé   8 x 6.5   1980. Limited edition of 200

246 Bookplate for P. & D. Colnaghi   7.5 x 10   1980
Limited edition of 100

247 Bookplate for Iain Bain   10.75 x 7.25   1980
Limited edition of 80

248 Bookplate for Adrian Sassoon   7.25 x 10   1980
Limited edition of 100

249 Bookplate for Mr and Mrs Ely   10.25 x 7.75   1980
Limited edition of 70

250 Winfrith Court for Anthony Jaggard   7 x 10.5   1980
Limited edition of 80

251 Frontispiece 'Rhinoceros Beetle'   12 x 9.5   1978
Pearwood. For *Buzz Buzz*, poems by John Heath-Stubbs, Gruffyground Press, 1981. Limited edition of 100, 1978

252 The artist's cats   3.5 x 5.75   1981
Limited edition of 100

253 Small bookplate for Iain Bain   4.75 x 6.75   1983
Limited edition of 100

254 Bookplate for John Loch   10.25 x 7.75   1983
Limited edition of 100

255 Bookplate for Anne Stevens   11.25 x 7.5   1983
Limited edition of 100

256 Bookplate for Benoît Junod   9 x 7.25   1983
Limited edition of 100

257-258 Two engravings for *Vines* by D. Burnett, Rocket Press, 1984
Limited edition of 100 each of: Thais   9 x 6.25
                                Girl's Head   7.25 x 6.25

Second editions of 50 to accompany special copies of the book (Roman numerals)

259 Bookplate for Brian North Lee   12 x 9.5   1984
Limited edition of 100

260 Bookplate for John C. Bullitt   7.75 x 9   1984
Limited edition of 100

261 Bookplate for Oswald Cheung   9 x 7.5   1984
Limited edition of 100

262 Bookplate for Raymond and Pamela Lister   8.75 x 6.5   1984. Limited edition of 100

263 Bookplate for David Profumo   9.5 x 8   1984.
Limited edition of 100

264 Colophon for Collins Harvill   4.5 x 2.75   1984

18 engravings, engraved between 1977 and 1983, for *Messer Pietro Mio* were published in 1985 by the Libanus Press. Limited edition of 100. Circa 25 Solander cases with printed labels containing 17 engravings in 12 mounts were made.

265 Flower decoration   4.5 x 4.5

266 Hands   2 x 5.25

267 Altar   5.75 x 4.5

268 'f.f.' Cornucopias   7.75 x 5.75

269 Agnus Dei   7.5 x 5

270 Putti   6 x 9.5

271 L P Cartouche   3.5 x 5

272 Bembo funerary arms   6 x 9.25

273 Lucrezia Borgia   7.75 x 5.25

274 Pietro Bembo   7.75 x 4.75

275 Decorated rule   1 x 8.5

276 Arms of Pope Leo X   6.25 x 10.25

277 Preface   4.5 x 11

278 Este Tomb   7 x 11.25

279 Triumph of Death   7.5 x 11.25

280 Lucrezia mourning   7.75 x 11

281 Heart pendant   4.75 x 3.5

282 Scallop   2 x 2.75

283 Two Fantastics   12 x 9   1984   Pearwood

284 Bookplate for Mrs H. Keswick   11 x 7.5   1988
Limited edition of 100

4 chapter headings for Julian Berry   5.5 x 9.5   1989
for *Enchanting Paths to Paradise* by C. Thacker (unpublished) St Barnabas Press. Limited edition of 100 of each

285 Painshill

286 Stourhead

287 Fonthill Splendens

288 Fonthill Abbey

MAIN EXHIBITIONS

Mount Gallery, Hampstead: one man show of paintings, collages and engravings, 1963

Waterhouse Gallery, London W2: first one man show of paintings, collages and engravings, 1971

Waterhouse Gallery, London W2: second one man show of collages and engravings, 1973

Oxford Gallery: first one man show of collages, paintings and engravings, 1976

Durham University: one man show of paintings, collages and illustrated books, 1977

Borough of Thamesdown Museum and Art Gallery, Swindon: 'Eight Figurative Painters', group exhibition, 1977

Oxford Gallery: second one man show of wood engravings and paintings, 1978

International Ex Libris Centre, Belgium: group exhibition with Joan Hassall, Reynolds Stone and Leo Wyatt: wood engravings, 1978

Blewbury Festival: one man show of paintings and engravings featuring the Libanus Press, 1979

Kings Arms Yard, Dorchester, Dorset: one man show of paintings, montages and engravings, 1980

Oxford Gallery: third one man show of paintings, montages and engravings, 1980

Medici Gallery, London W1: group exhibition with 'British Wood Engravers', 1980

Blewbury Festival: one man show of paintings and engravings and the painted clavichord made by Sir Evelyn Shuckburgh, 1981

Katharine House Gallery, Marlborough: first one man show mostly of mural studies, 1982

Borlase Gallery, Blewbury: one man show of montages, studies for mural decorations, paintings and wood engravings, 1982

Katharine House Gallery, Marlborough: second one man show of mural studies, 1983

Harrow School: group exhibition with Reynolds Stone, Leo Wyatt, Peter Reddick and George Tute: wood engravings, 1983

Eton College: one man show of mural studies and wood engravings, 1984

Parkin Gallery, London W1: group exhibition 'The Artist as Illustrator' wood engravings, 1984

Richard Shirley Smith Fiftieth Birthday Retrospective Exhibition, 1985 *The Ashmolean Museum, McAlpine and Eldon Galleries*, Oxford & *RIBA Heinz Gallery*, 21 Portman Square, London W1

Aldeburgh Festival of Music & the Arts: one man show, wood engravings and mural cartoons, 1988

Galerie in der Mühle, Buxtehude W. Germany group exhibition, Six British Wood Engravers, 1990

Maas Gallery, London W1: one man show of Paintings and Engravings, 1992

Marlborough Festival, *Katharine House*, The Wood Engravings of Richard Shirley Smith and Simon Brett, 1992

MAIN ILLUSTRATED BOOKS

Wood engraved unless otherwise indicated

A Point of Departure by Joy Finzi, Golden Head Press, 1967 (engraved 1961)

When April Came by M. Burtch, Novello, 1962

'Aspects of Rome' in *Prospect* edited by Roger Bannister, Hutchinson, 1962

The Great Teresa by E. Hamilton, Burns and Oates (Universe Books edition), 1963

Of Flowers and a Village by Wilfrid Blunt, Hamish Hamilton, 1963 (line drawings)

The Golden Cantata poems Kathleen Raine, music Sir Arthur Bliss, Novello, 1933 (Monotype)

Pandora's Last Voyage by G. Rawson, Longmans, 1963

The English Church 1000 to 1066 by F. Barlow, Longmans, 1963

The Writings of St Francis of Assisi Burns and Oates, 1963

The Gourmet's Garden by D. Bartrum, Faber and Faber, 1964

To any Christian by a Benedictine of Stanbrook, Burns and Oates, 1964

The Darkening Green by E. Clarke, Faber and Faber, 1964

A Street in Suffolk by Adrian Bell, Faber & Faber, 1964 (monotype and line drawings)

Helmet and Wasps by M. Mott, Andre Deutsch, 1964

The Trial of Thomas More by E.E. Reynolds, Burns and Oates, 1964

Metamorphoses by Ursula Vaughan Williams, Duckworth, 1965

A Fool in the Forest by Leonard Clark, Dobson, 1965 (monotypes)

False Colours by Georgette Heyer, Longmans, 1965

The Folio Society prospectus, 1965

The Faith of Teilhard de Chardin by H. de Lubac, Burns and Oates, 1965

Thomas More and Erasmus by E.E. Reynolds, Burns and Oates, 1965

Margaret Clitherow by M. Claridge, Burns and Oates, 1965

Sir Roger de Coverly by Addison and Steele, The Folio Society, 1967

Masters of Music (series) Percy M.Young (line drawings and monotype cover) Handel 1965, Mozart 1965, Beethoven 1966, Britten 1966, Debussy 1968, Tchaikovsky 1968, Hayden 1969, Stravinsky 1969

Memoirs of a London Doll by R.H. Horne, Andre Deutsch, 1967

Garland, an anthology, Golden Head Press, 1968

The Prince and the Puppeteer by J.C. Bretherton, Compton Press, 1969 (lino cut)

Hero and Leander by David Burnett, published privately, 1975 (lino cuts made in 1969)

Cover designs for *The Periodical* (Quarterly) Oxford University Press, 1970

The Poems of Percy Bysshe Shelley selected by Stephen Spender for the Limited Editions Club of New York, 1971

Letters to His Son by the Earl of Chesterfield, The Folio Society, 1973

The River Boy by Theresa Whistler, Oxford University Press, 1976 (line drawings)

The Closed Door by James Reeves, Gruffyground Press, 1977

Six Hampshire Epitaphs Gruffyground Press, 1977 (unpublished)

Buzz Buzz, Ten Insect Poems by John Heath-Stubbs, Gruffyground Press, 1981

Selected Engravings of Richard Shirley Smith 1960-77, introduction by Laurence Whistler, Cuckoo Hill Press, 1983

Vines by David Burnett, Rocket Press, 1984

Messer Pietro Mio correspondence of Lucrezia Borgia and Pietro Bembo, Translated by Hugh Shankland, Libanus Press, 1985

The Testament of Charlotte B edited by M. Kociejowski, Libanus Press 1988 (line drawings)

Enchanting Paths to Paradise, by Christopher Thacker (5 paintings, 4 engravings) St Barnabas Press 1992 (unpublished)

The Dramatic Monologues, by Robert Browning, introduction by A.S. Byatt, The Folio Society, 1991 (line drawings)

Perfect and Imperfect Enjoyments, The Earl of Rochester's Poems The Folio Society 1992. This being their first signed & numbered Limited Edition (8 paintings)

The Boke of Iford by Harold A. Peto, Introduction by Robin Whalley, Libanus Press, 1993 (line drawings)

The Wood Engravings of Richard Shirley Smith, Selected & introduced by Iain Bain, Silent Books, 1993

ILLUSTRATED PERIODICAL
& NEWSPAPER ARTICLES

Waterhouse Gallery Exhibition by Marina Vaizey. The Financial Times, July 15 1971

Palladio's Venice brought to life by Simon Brett, The Times Educational Supplement, January 1974

People into Buildings by the editor, Architectural Review, Vol. CLXI, 1977

Bookplate Designs of Richard Shirley Smith by Brian North Lee, The Private Library, Vol. 10, 1977

Wall to wall paintings by Lucy Hughes-Hallett, Vogue, March 1 1979

An Eye for the Rich and Unreal by Diana Winsor, Telegraph Sunday Magazine, No. 206, September 7 1980

Unique painted clavichord, Antique Collector, August 1982

Richard Shirley Smith und seine Holzstich-Exlibris by Brian North Lee, Österreichisches Jahrbuch für Ex Libris etc. 1981-1982 Band 53

Profile of an Artist: Richard Shirley Smith by David Chambers, The Bookplate Journal, Vol. 3 No. 1, March 1985

Some New Works with Italian Inspiration by Elizabeth Williamson, Daily Telegraph, Sept: 3 1985

Richard Shirley Smith. The Ashmolean, Number Eight, Autumn 1985

My First Fifty Years Country Life, September 12 1985

Richard Shirley Smith by Megan Tressidder, The World of Interiors, October 1985

Renaissance Man by Isabelle Anscombe, Observer, October 6 1985

The Painter as Wood Engraver by Linda Saunders, The Green Book, Vol. 2 No.1, Autumn 1985

Richard Shirley Smith: Paintings, Collages and Murals by Henry Ford, in the Fiftieth Birthday Retrospective Catalogue, 1985

Richard Shirley Smith as a Wood Engraver by Brian North Lee, in the Fiftieth Birthday Retrospective Catalogue, 1985

The Enchantment of Decay and Melancholia by Sir Roy Strong, Financial Times, November 21 1985

Review of Selected Engravings Fine Print No.4, October 1985

Exhibition of Work at the Ashmolean Museum, Oxford by Simon Brett. Society of Wood-engravers Journal, No. 2, 1986

A Curious Art by Rachel Sylvester, Telegraph Magazine, 9 May 1992

A Perfectionist by Nature by Lindsay Fulcher, The Lady, 5-11 May 1992

Richard Shirley Smith by John Russell Taylor, Maas Gallery Catalogue for 1992 Exhibition

Rodney Armstrong Fund Plate, A.S. Arellanes (Ed), Bookplates in the News, No.89, July 1992, California USA

Text & Image by David Burnett, Scottish Book Collector, Vol. 3 No.6, August-September 1992